RAPTURE SURVIVAL GUIDE

L. Bohm

Published by L. Bohm

Copyright 2015 L. Bohm

Rapture Survival Guide

Table of Contents

What is the Rapture?

First, what is the Rapture? The Rapture is meant for the church age, the time from Pentecost until the present time. The Christians that have believed in Jesus and trusted Him for their salvation will be caught up to heaven and given their incorruptible bodies. Even the ones that have been in the grave, or have been cremated will be given their perfect bodies at this time. These Christians will be taken out of the world in preparation of the Tribulation period that is to come. God will be sending down judgments on the world in a last effort to get the attention of non-believers. The ones left behind after the rapture are not lost; they still have a chance to turn to God and to trust Jesus for their salvation. They will have to endure the horrors of the Tribulation period, but even if they die during this time, they will be with Christ.

Many people say that the word "rapture" does not occur in the Bible at all, but neither does the trinity or even the word Bible. If you go back to the original translation, the Latin word "rapere" was translated from the Greek word "harpazo", which means "caught up"; it became commonly known as the Rapture. Many people say that the church did not start preaching about the Rapture until Reverend Morgan Edwards in 1742. There is a writing from 373 AD in which Ephraim the Syrian had been writing about the Rapture.

"For all the saints and the elect of God are gathered prior to the Tribulation that is to come,and are taken to the Lord, lest they see the confusion that is to overwhelm the world because of our sin."

The pre-tribulation rapture was widely preached up until the Council of Ephesus declared it heretical in 431 AD. It only began to be taught again during the reform movement of the seventeenth century.

Another reason for the pre-tribulation view is these verses in 2 Thessalonians 2, where Paul was writing to the church at Thessalonica. They were concerned about missing the second coming of Jesus; Paul reminds them of the things that he has taught them.

2 Concerning the coming of our Lord Jesus Christ and our being gathered to him, we ask you, brothers and sisters, 2 not to become easily unsettled or alarmed by the teaching allegedly from us—whether by a prophecy or by word of mouth or by letter—asserting that the day of the Lord has already come. 3 Don't let anyone deceive you in any way, for that day will not come until the rebellion occurs and the man of lawlessness is revealed, the man doomed to destruction. 4 He will oppose and will exalt himself over everything that is called God or is worshiped, so that he sets himself up in God's temple, proclaiming himself to be God. 5 Don't you remember that when I was with you I used to tell you these things? 6 And now you know what is holding him back, so that he may be revealed at the proper time. 7 For the secret power of lawlessness is already at work; but the one who now holds it back will continue to do so till he is taken out of the way. 8 And then the lawless one will be revealed, whom the Lord Jesus will overthrow with the breath of his mouth and destroy by the splendor of his coming. 9 The coming of the lawless one will be in accordance with how Satan works. He will use all sorts of displays of power through signs and wonders that serve the lie, 10 and all the ways that wickedness deceives those who are perishing. They perish because they refused to love the truth and so be saved. 11 For this reason God sends them a powerful delusion so that they will believe the lie 12 and so that all will be condemned who have not believed the truth but have delighted in wickedness.   2 Thessalonians 2:1-12

Jesus will not return before the man of lawlessness is revealed, which is the Antichrist. There is something that is holding him back from being revealed and that is the Holy Spirit that was sent down to be with believers at Pentecost. When the Holy Spirit was sent to the believers his purpose was to teach them and transform them to lead a godly life. Receiving the spirit is also a sign from God that we are part of the family of God and the Spirit enables us to be witnesses to others about the truth of Jesus Christ and salvation through Him.

22 But the fruit of the Spirit is love, joy, peace, forbearance, kindness, goodness, faithfulness, 23 gentleness and self-control. Against such things there is no law. 24 Those who belong to Christ Jesus have crucified the flesh with its passions and desires. 25 Since we live by the Spirit, let us keep in step with the Spirit. Galatians 5:22-25

15 "If you love me, keep my commands. 16 And I will ask the Father, and he will give you another advocate to help you and be with you forever— 17 the Spirit of truth. The world cannot accept him, because it neither sees him nor knows him. But you know him, for he lives with you and will be in you. 18 I will not leave you as orphans; I will come to you. 19 Before long, the world will not see me anymore, but you will see me. Because I live, you also will live. 20 On that day you will realize that I am in my Father, and you are in me, and I am in you. 21 Whoever has my commands and keeps them is the one who loves me. The one who loves me will be loved by my Father, and I too will love them and show myself to them." 22 Then Judas (not Judas Iscariot) said, "But, Lord, why do you intend to show yourself to us and not to the world?" 23 Jesus replied, "Anyone who loves me will obey my teaching. My Father will love them, and we will come to them and make our home with them. 24 Anyone who does not love me will not obey my teaching. These words you hear are not my own; they belong to the Father who sent me. 25 "All this I have spoken while still with you. 26 But the Advocate, the Holy Spirit, whom the Father will send in my name, will teach you all things and will remind you of everything I have said to you. 27 Peace I leave with you; my peace I give you. I do not give to you as the world gives. Do not let your hearts be troubled and do not be afraid. 28 "You heard me say, 'I am going away and I am coming back to you.' If you loved me, you would be glad that I am going to the Father, for the Father is greater than I. 29 I have told you now before it happens, so that when it does happen you will believe. 30 I will not say much more to you, for the prince of this world is coming. He has no hold over me, 31 but he

comes so that the world may learn that I love the Father
and do exactly what my Father has commanded me.
"Come now; let us leave. John 14:15-31

As you can see in these verses, Jesus promised to send the Holy Spirit to believers; to be with them forever. In the verses from 2 Thessalonians Paul reminds the believers that the Antichrist will not be revealed until the one that holds him back, the Holy Spirit, is removed from the world. Now God never lies, so when the Holy Spirit is removed from the world that would have to mean the believers are removed as well which confirms the pre-tribulation rapture view.

What will happen when the Rapture occurs? Many people know that the people that believed in Jesus for their salvation will be taken up to heaven.

13 Brothers and sisters, we do not want you to be
uninformed about those who sleep in death, so that you do
not grieve like the rest of mankind, who have no hope. 14
For we believe that Jesus died and rose again, and so we
believe that God will bring with Jesus those who have
fallen asleep in him. 15According to the Lord's word, we

tell you that we who are still alive, who are left until the coming of the Lord, will certainly not precede those who have fallen asleep. 16 For the Lord himself will come down from heaven, with a loud command, with the voice of the archangel and with the trumpet call of God, and the dead in Christ will rise first. 17 After that, we who are still alive and are left will be caught up together with them in the clouds to meet the Lord in the air. And so we will be with the Lord forever. 18 Therefore encourage one another with these words.1 Thessalonians 4:13-18

51 Listen, I tell you a mystery: We will not all sleep, but we will all be changed— 52 in a flash, in the twinkling of an eye, at the last trumpet. For the trumpet will sound, the dead will be raised imperishable, and we will be changed. 53 For the perishable must clothe itself with the imperishable, and the mortal with immortality. 1 Corinthians 15:51-53

1 "Do not let your hearts be troubled. You believe in God; believe also in me. 2 My Father's house has many rooms; if that were not so, would I have told you that I am going there to prepare a place for you? 3 And if I go and prepare a place for you, I will come back and take you to be with me that you also may be where I am. John 14:1-3

7Therefore you do not lack any spiritual gift as you eagerly wait for our Lord Jesus Christ to be revealed. 8 He will also keep you firm to the end, so that you will be blameless on the day of our Lord Jesus Christ. 1 Corinthians 1:7-8

The coming wrath would be the Tribulation that will come upon the earth once the church is removed. *9 For God did not appoint us to suffer wrath but to receive salvation through our Lord Jesus Christ. 1 Thessalonians 5:9*

13 while we wait for the blessed hope—the appearing of the glory of our great God and Savior, Jesus Christ. Titus 2:13

The Blessed Hope is another name for the Rapture. It is what we look forward to so that we do not have to suffer through the Tribulation period where God will unleash His wrath on the earth and so we can be with Jesus.

10 Since you have kept my command to endure patiently, I will also keep you from the hour of trial that is going to come on the whole world to test the inhabitants of the earth. Revelation 3:10

This is from the beginning of Revelation, it is from the letter John is told to write to the Church in Philadelphia. The seven letters that John writes are to specific churches of his time, but they are also written to modern church types. The Church in Philadelphia is doing what is right and not trusting false prophets, they are true believers, God tells them that He will keep them from the hour of Tribulation. This applies to all true Christians that have trusted Jesus for their salvation. In this is verse we are told that we, the church, are to be saved from the Tribulation. That does not mean that Christians do not suffer tribulations and trials while we are on the earth. God never claims that we will be exempt from these things, but it is a promise that we will not have to suffer the final seven years of the Tribulation when God will pour out His wrath, like nothing you have ever seen or experienced.

To sum it up, the rapture is the event that ends the church age, or the age of grace. Once the rapture has occurred the Antichrist will rise up and take control of the world, his signing of the peace treaty with Israel will be the start of the Tribulation period. These seven years will be the worst that the world has ever seen, but take hope, after this time Jesus will return. After the rapture there may be some time before the Tribulation begins, it could begin within a few days or weeks or even years. The defining point of the Tribulation is the signing of the peace treaty with Israel, that is the official start of the Tribulation.

You may wonder why there is a rapture or a tribulation to come. It all starts with Israel; they were disobedient to God and chose to worship idols. They also ignored God's command to work the land for six years and for the seventh let it rest; this is called the Shmita or the Sabbath year. The Jewish people did not obey God and continued to plant and work the land. God sent prophets like Elijah to warn the people to give up these idols and return to worshipping the one true God. The people ignored him and as punishment God let the Israelites be carried off by other lands like the Assyrians and the Babylonians. Not everyone worshipped idols, good men like Daniel prayed fervently for the return of the people to their land. God sent Daniel prophetic dreams that included the timeline for Israel to return to their homeland.

24 "Seventy 'sevens' are decreed for your people and your holy city to finish transgression, to put an end to sin, to atone for wickedness, to bring in everlasting righteousness, to seal up vision and prophecy and to anoint the Most Holy Place. 25 "Know and understand this: From the time the word goes out to restore and rebuild Jerusalem until the Anointed One, the ruler, comes, there will be seven 'sevens,' and sixty-two 'sevens.' It will be rebuilt with streets and a trench, but in times of trouble. 26 After the sixty-two 'sevens,' the Anointed One will be put to death and will have nothing. The people of the ruler who will come will destroy the city and the sanctuary. The end will come like a flood: War will continue until the end, and desolations have been decreed. 27 He will confirm a covenant with many for one 'seven.' In the middle of the 'seven' he will put an end to sacrifice and offering. And at the temple he will set up an abomination that causes desolation, until the end that is decreed is poured out on him." Daniel 9:24-27

The prophecy gave 70 weeks for their return, now the weeks represented years. One year for every year the Israelites ignored the Shmita. After the 69th week, Jesus came as the Messiah for Israel. The Jews rejected Him as their Messiah and He was crucified. Before His crucifixion, Jesus began to minister to the gentiles and they accepted Him as their savior and the Son of God. At the point that Jesus was rejected by the Jews the countdown stopped, in this interim period is the church age, the age we are living in now. We accept the gift of salvation that Jesus died to give to us and by grace we are saved from death; not a physical death, but a spiritual one. Once the rapture occurs and the church is taken to be with Jesus the 70th week will begin. This last seven years God is focusing on Israel, all the tribulations that will befall the earth are God's last effort to reach Israel. This time it will work, Israel will finally see that they rejected their Messiah all those years ago. God will send two witnesses to preach the truth to the Jews and 144.000 from the twelve tribes of Israel will rise up and preach the truth to the world and millions of Jews will finally turn to God. It will be impossible not to believe during this time, the hand of God will be so obvious that there will no longer be any atheists left on the earth.

When Will the Rapture Happen?

No one really knows when the rapture will occur. All we can do is look out for the signs that Jesus said will happen during the beginning of the end times.

3 As Jesus was sitting on the Mount of Olives, the disciples came to him privately. "Tell us," they said, "when will this happen, and what will be the sign of your coming and of the end of the age?" 4 Jesus answered: "Watch out that no one deceives you. 5 For many will come in my name, claiming, 'I am the Messiah,' and will deceive many. 6 You will hear of wars and rumors of wars, but see to it that you are not alarmed. Such things must happen, but the end is still to come. 7 Nation will rise against nation, and kingdom against kingdom. There will be famines and earthquakes in various places. 8 All these are the beginning of birth pains. Matthew 24:3-8 (NIV)

3 But mark this: There will be terrible times in the last days. 2 People will be lovers of themselves, lovers of money, boastful, proud, abusive, disobedient to their parents, ungrateful, unholy, 3 without love, unforgiving, slanderous, without self-control, brutal, not lovers of the good, 4 treacherous, rash, conceited, lovers of pleasure rather than lovers of God— 5 having a form of godliness but denying its power. Have nothing to do with such people. 2 Timothy 3:1-5 (NIV)

25 "There will be signs in the sun, moon and stars. On the earth, nations will be in anguish and perplexity at the roaring and tossing of the sea. 26 People will faint from terror, apprehensive of what is coming on the world, for the heavenly bodies will be shaken. 27 At that time they will see the Son of Man coming in a cloud with power and great glory. 28 When these things begin to take place, stand up and lift up your heads, because your redemption is drawing near." Luke 21:25-28 (NIV)

Reading these verses causes me to think about the times we are living in. All these things have happened or are happening, the signs are there. It is only a matter of time before the rapture occurs. Jesus said that these are the beginnings of the birth pangs, now you know that when a woman goes into labor the contractions start slow and far apart, and as it gets closer to the time that she will give birth the contractions grow stronger and closer together. Read the news, look at the headlines, there are all sorts of events that seem to be happening more and more and the disasters are getting stronger. Look at the catastrophic earthquakes that have been happening, the planet has at least one or more earthquakes stronger than a 6.0 magnitude every week. Look at the hurricanes that have occurred in the last 20 years, Katrina, Rita, Andrew, Sandy and these are only some of the hurricanes not counting the ones that strike other countries. I write a weekly disaster blog at http://devastationanddisaster.wordpress.com, the amount of disasters that occur all over the world is alarming. This year there have been so many major storms all over the world that have caused catastrophic flooding and much loss of life and property. The birth pangs are getting stronger, we are told to watch, and through my disaster blog I am watching what is unfolding around the world and I am always ready for the rapture. If you discount the disasters all you need to do is look at the behavior of the people. There have always been murders since the time that Cain killed Abel, but I have noticed that more and more murders have been occurring, parents don't care about their children and abuse them or allow them to be abused, and children kill their parents for the smallest offenses. People care only about themselves and their pleasures, look how popular the "selfie" has become, people are vain and arrogant. Look at what is on TV and what is on the radio, every commandment has been broken and Satanism and witchcraft and violence are so prevalent that most people don't even notice anymore. We have become desensitized to murder and violence and all sorts of evil. We accept all these things as normal and the family unit is being ripped apart. These are all signs that the end is coming soon.

There are other signs that Jesus gave, He said that knowledge would increase and you only have to look at history to see how much the world has changed technologically in the last 100 years. More than any other time in history we have made more technological advancements than the entire history before. We have cars and planes and computers, knowledge is at our fingertips. A trip that would have taken weeks or months now takes a few hours. Technology has now gotten to the point that parts of the end time prophecies are achievable. One instance is where the two witnesses are killed and lie in the street for three days and the whole world saw them, with satellite and internet that is now possible. We can easily see what is going on around the world with a few taps of our fingers.

8 Their bodies will lie in the public square of the great city—which is figuratively called Sodom and Egypt—where also their Lord was crucified. 9 For three and a half days

some from every people, tribe, language and nation will
gaze on their bodies and refuse them burial. Revelation
11:8-9

Another example of technology that has reached the level required to fulfill prophecy is the mark of the beast. Many think this may be a microchip that will be implanted and that technology is now available. Many people have already accepted having this chip implanted into their bodies and there is discussion about implanting children when they are born. Right now getting a chip is a voluntary thing, but one day it will not be. Another option in development is an electronic tattoo, this is not a real tattoo, right now it is similar to a fake tattoo. Its primary use will be in medicine but this may eventually lead to permanent implantation. There are probably be other inventions that will come along before the time of the mark of the beast but you can see that the basic technology is already there.

You may see people, even famous preachers that say that they have figured out the exact day that the rapture will happen. They announce it and write books about it and when it does not happen they say they must have miscalculated. These are false preachers and when they predict a date and the rapture does not come people stop believing and are pushed away from God. If you have watched the news Harold Camping made several predictions for the rapture using his calculations, none of them came true. No one knows the day that the rapture will happen but God.

36 "But about that day or hour no one knows, not even the angels in heaven, nor the Son, but only the Father. 37 As it was in the days of Noah, so it will be at the coming of the Son of Man. 38 For in the days before the flood, people were eating and drinking, marrying and giving in marriage, up to the day Noah entered the ark; 39 and they knew nothing about what would happen until the flood came and took them all away. That is how it will be at the coming of the Son of Man. 40 Two men will be in the field; one will be taken and the other left. 41 Two women will be grinding with a hand mill; one will be taken and the other left. 42 "Therefore keep watch, because you do not know on what day your Lord will come. 43 But understand this: If the owner of the house had known at what time of night the thief was coming, he would have kept watch and would not have let his house be broken into. 44 So you also must be ready, because the Son of Man will come at an hour when you do not expect him. Matthew 24:36-44

Even Jesus did not know when the day would be, He said only God knows. If Jesus did not know, do you really think someone could "figure it out"????? We are only told about the signs that Jesus would be returning for His church so that we may be ready.

According to these verses, the Rapture will come at an unexpected time. I believe that this proves that the Rapture will have to come before the Tribulation period. If it were to happen at any other time, like mid-tribulation or post-tribulation, then it would not be unexpected. We would be looking for it to happen at a specific point. The only way these verses can make sense is if the Rapture occurs before the Tribulation.

7 He said to them: "It is not for you to know the times or dates the Father has set by his own authority. Acts 1:7

36 "But about that day or hour no one knows, not even the angels in heaven, nor the Son, but only the Father. 37 As it was in the days of Noah, so it will be at the coming of the Son of Man. 38 For in the days before the flood, people were eating and drinking, marrying and giving in marriage, up to the day Noah entered the ark; 39 and they knew nothing about what would happen until the flood came and took them all away. That is how it will be at the coming of the Son of Man. 40 Two men will be in the field; one will be taken and the other left.41 Two women will be grinding with a hand mill; one will be taken and the other left. 42 "Therefore keep watch, because you do not know on what day your Lord will come. 43 But understand this: If the owner of the house had known at what time of night the thief was coming, he would have kept watch and would not have let his house be broken into. 44 So you also must be ready, because the Son of Man will come at an hour when you do not expect him. 45 "Who then is the faithful and wise servant, whom the master has put in charge of the servants in his household to give them their food at the proper time? 46 It will be good for that servant whose master finds him doing so when he returns. 47 Truly I tell you, he will put him in charge of all his possessions.48 But suppose that servant is wicked and says to himself, 'My master is staying away a long time,' 49 and he then begins to beat his fellow servants and to eat and drink with drunkards. 50 The master of that servant will come on a day when he does not expect him and at an hour he is not aware of. 51 He will cut him to pieces and assign him a place with the hypocrites, where there will be weeping and gnashing of teeth. Matthew 24:36-51

"At that time the kingdom of heaven will be like ten virgins who took their lamps and went out to meet the bridegroom. 2 Five of them were foolish and five were wise. 3 The foolish ones took their lamps but did not take any oil with them. 4 The wise ones, however, took oil in jars along with their lamps. 5 The bridegroom was a long time in coming, and they all became drowsy and fell asleep. 6 "At midnight the cry rang out: 'Here's the bridegroom! Come out to meet him!' 7 "Then all the virgins woke up and trimmed their lamps. 8 The foolish ones said to the wise, 'Give us some of your oil; our lamps are going out.' 9 "'No,' they replied, 'there may not be enough for both us and you. Instead, go to those who sell oil and buy some for yourselves.' 10 "But while they were on their way to buy the oil, the bridegroom arrived. The virgins who were ready went in with him to the wedding banquet. And the door was shut. 11 "Later the others also came. 'Lord, Lord,' they said, 'open the door for us!' 12 "But he replied, 'Truly I tell you, I don't know you.' 13 "Therefore keep watch, because you do not know the day or the hour" Matthew 25:1-13

What If I Am Left Behind?

One morning you wake up, it is a beautiful day and you have so much to do today. You get out of bed and get ready for the day; you get into your car and start driving to your destination. Maybe you are going to work, or you are on vacation or it is the weekend, nothing seems different about today. As you drive you see people going about their business, they are heading to work or doing some shopping, you drive past a church where someone just got married. It is a day the same as any other, or so it seems…you pull into your favorite donut shop to get some coffee, as you reach out to hand the cashier your money she disappears. At first you can't believe your eyes, what just happened? Then you hear other people professing shock that the person next to them has disappeared, mothers are frantically looking for their children who just disappeared, and everyone is looking around with a shocked expression. Now you start hearing cars crashing and people screaming from outside, you see driverless cars that have crashed and others looking for their passengers. You hear a noise and look up; a plane seems to be falling from the sky. You run to your car to try to get home but there is so much chaos all around you that there is nowhere safe or clear to drive. You begin to walk home, seeing more destruction and people running all over the place, terrified, looking for loved ones. After a long time you finally make it home, you try to call your family, if you can get through you will find that some are gone, and all the children are gone, but some are not. You turn on the TV to see if there is any answer to what happened, it seems that there is chaos on every channel, and some channels seem to be off the air completely. From what you can tell it looks like this event happened all over the world. As you stare mindlessly at the TV and hope for answers something is nagging at you, something about all this seems familiar. Maybe you had been to church when you were younger, or had someone in your family try to tell you about God at some point. You may have read something somewhere or even seen something on TV or in a movie, but you remember something about disappearances in the Bible. You get on your computer, if you have electricity, or maybe you have a Bible collecting dust somewhere, or maybe you head down to a church to see if anyone is there. Then you see it, something called the rapture. It seems to describe everything that you saw today. After reading everything you can find, you finally realize that you missed it...what does that mean for you? Are you doomed? Is there a second chance? You fall down on your knees and you beg God to give you another chance, to take you too. You feel comforted after praying and you decide to head to the nearest church to see if anyone is there and if you can find more information. Most of the people in that church had been raptured, but there were others like you, they knew they missed it and were crying out to God. After talking with some of the members you learn that there is a second chance, but that you will have to endure all the judgments that are going to come, and you may even be killed because of your new faith. It is a lot to take in for a new believer but you realize that this is your only hope. It feels right and you feel the presence of God. More and more people are coming to the church; many of them are choosing to follow God, some walk away in disbelief. All the new believers gather together daily to pray and to learn more about what is to come. God laid it all out in the book of Revelation. You learn that a leader would rise up that comes to power on a platform of peace; the world is in chaos and gratefully follows this man. At first it seems that he is doing a great job, he is getting things under control and the world economy is stabilizing. To bring order to the economies of the world he institutes a one world currency. He even proposes a reason for the disappearances and the world is deceived and believes him. He speaks about unity and the fact that one thing keeps the world from being unified and causes the most strife, that is religion. A one world religion is proposed, the world agrees that this is a smart move. Then this man will do what no one else could, he brings peace to the Middle East, he signs a peace treaty with Israel for seven years. Everyone will be lauding this man as the greatest leader the world has ever known, but know the truth; the signing of this peace treaty is the beginning of Daniel's 70th week and the beginning of the Tribulation. What happens now? One by one Jesus will release the judgments onto this world, first the seven seals, then the seven trumpets and finally the seven bowls. After all these judgments have come to pass, Jesus will return to earth to fight the final battle of Armageddon on the plain of Har Megiddo. If you make it to the end of these seven years, you will have endured suffering and disaster that the world has never seen. You will be persecuted for your beliefs, possible beheaded if you refuse to take the mark of the beast at the midpoint of the tribulation, but stand fast, even if you die you will be taken immediately to the throne of God and join the martyrs that come out of the tribulation.

9 When he opened the fifth seal, I saw under the altar the souls of those who had been slain because of the word of God and the testimony they had maintained. 10 They called out in a loud voice, "How long, Sovereign Lord, holy and true, until you judge the inhabitants of the earth and avenge our blood?"11 Then each of them was given a white robe, and they were told to wait a little longer, until

the full number of their fellow servants, their brothers and sisters, were killed just as they had been. Revelation 6:9-11

This will be the worst time in history; nothing that you have ever seen or experienced will prepare you for what is to come. Have faith in God and pray often, join with other believers and band together to help each other.

The Seven Seals

The rapture has occurred, the Antichrist has risen onto the world scene and the peace treaty has been signed with Israel. The Tribulation has officially begun and Jesus Christ, the Lamb of God is about to open the first seal that will release the first judgment.

I watched as the Lamb opened the first of the seven seals. Then I heard one of the four living creatures say in a voice like thunder, "Come!" 2 I looked, and there before me was a white horse! Its rider held a bow, and he was given a crown, and he rode out as a conqueror bent on conquest.3 When the Lamb opened the second seal, I heard the second living creature say, "Come!" 4 Then another horse came out, a fiery red one. Its rider was given power to take peace from the earth and to make people kill each other. To him was given a large sword.5 When the Lamb opened the third seal, I heard the third living creature say, "Come!" I looked, and there before me was a black horse! Its rider was holding a pair of scales in his hand. 6 Then I heard what sounded like a voice among the four living creatures, saying, "Two pounds of wheat for a day's wages,[and six pounds of barley for a day's wages, and do not damage the oil and the wine!"7 When the Lamb opened the fourth seal, I heard the voice of the fourth living creature say,

"Come!" 8 I looked, and there before me was a pale horse! Its rider was named Death, and Hades was following close behind him. They were given power over a fourth of the earth to kill by sword, famine and plague, and by the wild beasts of the earth. Revelation 6:1-8

Now this may sound familiar to you, I think everyone has heard of the four horsemen of the apocalypse; this is where the concept came from. The first horse is the white horse; its rider has a bow and a crown and is out to conquer. This rider will conquer through a false peace, he holds a bow but no arrows, and he will rise to power proclaiming peace. We know this rider represents the Antichrist who comes to power on a platform of peace and goodwill but in reality his aim is to rule the world. The second horse is red and he stands for war. He follows the white rider and helps him in his rise to power; anyone that stands against the white rider will feel his sword. The third rider is the black horse and its rider holds scales, this horseman stands for famine. Food for one person for a day will cost the day's wages and many will starve, he is told not to touch the oil and wine because the world's elite will get rich on the world's misfortune. The fourth seal releases the pale horse that stands for Death, and Hades is following behind him. It only makes sense that this horseman follows behind the others. They are given the power to kill one fourth of the earth by sword, famine, plague and the wild beasts. You may see these as horrible judgments, but they are just the beginning and not the worst that will be coming.

9 When he opened the fifth seal, I saw under the altar the souls of those who had been slain because of the word of God and the testimony they had maintained. 10 They called out in a loud voice, "How long, Sovereign Lord, holy and true, until you judge the inhabitants of the earth and avenge our blood?"11 Then each of them was given a white robe, and they were told to wait a little longer, until the full number of their fellow servants, their brothers and sisters, were killed just as they had been. Revelation 6:9-11

Once the horsemen have been released, Jesus opens the fifth seal. John sees an altar in heaven, and under the altar all those that had been killed for following Christ have become martyrs. They cry out, asking when will the inhabitants of the earth be judged for what they had done and when will their sacrifice be avenged. They are given the white robes of the martyr and told to wait for all the other martyrs that would be killed during the Tribulation period. God is just and merciful; He will not institute judgment until everyone is given a chance to turn to Him, but He will avenge the deaths of His people at the end of the Tribulation.

12 I watched as he opened the sixth seal. There was a great earthquake. The sun turned black like sackcloth made of goat hair, the whole moon turned blood red, 13 and the stars in the sky fell to earth, as figs drop from a fig tree when shaken by a strong wind. 14 The heavens receded like a scroll being rolled up, and every mountain and island was removed from its place.15 Then the kings of the earth, the princes, the generals, the rich, the mighty, and everyone else, both slave and free, hid in caves and among the rocks of the mountains. 16 They called to the mountains and the rocks, "Fall on us and hide us from the face of him who sits on the throne and from the wrath of the Lamb! 17 For the great day of their wrath has come, and who can withstand it?" Revelation 6:12-17

When Jesus opens the sixth seal, there is a huge earthquake. This earthquake was so large that every mountain and island was moved. The earthquake is felt all over the world and nowhere is safe. The sun turned black, the moon turned red and stars fell from the sky. This probably signifies an eclipse and meteors falling to earth.

31 The sun shall be turned to darkness, and the moon to blood, before the great and awesome day of the LORD comes. Joel 2:31

The peoples of the earth are terrified when this judgment occurs. They blame God for what is happening instead of repenting. They know that God is angry and that these are His judgments, but they will not give in and instead blame God and try to hide from his wrath. Before Jesus opens the seventh seal God gives an angel His seal, there are four angels holding back the four winds who are told to wait until God's seal was put on His servants. There were 12,000 sealed from each of the 12 tribes of Israel, these were to be protected from the wrath to come and they were to preach to the Jews about Jesus as the Messiah.

After this I saw four angels standing at the four corners of the earth, holding back the four winds of the earth to prevent any wind from blowing on the land or on the sea or on any tree. 2 Then I saw another angel coming up from the east, having the seal of the living God. He called out in a loud voice to the four angels who had been given power to harm the land and the sea: 3 "Do not harm the land or the sea or the trees until we put a seal on the foreheads of the servants of our God." 4 Then I heard the number of those who were sealed: 144,000 from all the tribes of Israel. Revelation 7:1-4

Now Jesus opens the seventh seal. There is silence in heaven for a half an hour. The first series of judgments is completed and the final seal ushers in the next judgments that are to come. This seal releases the seven angels who hold the seven trumpets that will be the next series of judgments. Another angel comes with a golden censer, he offers incense and the prayers of God's people on the altar in front of the throne, and then he fills it with fire and hurls it to the earth. This causes thunder, lightning and an earthquake.

When he opened the seventh seal, there was silence in heaven for about half an hour. 2 And I saw the seven angels who stand before God, and seven trumpets were given to them. 3 Another angel, who had a golden censer, came and stood at the altar. He was given much incense to offer, with the prayers of all God's people, on the golden altar in front of the throne. 4 The smoke of the incense, together with the prayers of God's people, went up before God from the angel's hand. 5 Then the angel took the censer, filled it with fire from the altar, and hurled it on the earth; and there came peals of thunder, rumblings, flashes of lightning and an earthquake. Revelation 8:1-5

The Seven Trumpets

The seven trumpets are the next series of judgments that will be poured out on the earth. The trumpets will be blown by the seven angels whose responsibility this is. Each successive judgment will be worse and contribute to the chaos on the earth. There can be no doubt in anyone's mind that these are the judgments of God, yet the people refuse to repent of their sins and acknowledge the one true God.

6 Then the seven angels who had the seven trumpets prepared to sound them. 7 The first angel sounded his trumpet, and there came hail and fire mixed with blood, and it was hurled down on the earth. A third of the earth was burned up, a third of the trees were burned up, and all the green grass was burned up. 8 The second angel sounded his trumpet, and something like a huge mountain, all ablaze, was thrown into the sea. A third of the sea turned into blood, 9 a third of the living creatures in the sea died, and a third of the ships were destroyed. 10 The third angel sounded his trumpet, and a great star, blazing like a torch, fell from the sky on a third of the rivers and on the springs of water— 11 the name of the star is Wormwood. A third of the waters turned bitter, and many people died from the waters that had become bitter. 12 The fourth angel sounded his trumpet, and a third of the sun was struck, a third of the moon, and a third of the stars, so that a third of them turned dark. A third of the day was without light, and also a third of the night. 13 As I watched, I heard an eagle that was flying in midair call out in a loud voice: "Woe! Woe! Woe to the inhabitants of the earth, because of the trumpet blasts about to be sounded by the other three angels!" Revelation 8:6-13

The first trumpet is blown and hail and fire mixed with blood are hurled down to the earth, one third of the earth was burned up including trees and grass. This is God's judgment on the land.   The second trumpet is blown, and it seemed like a huge mountain on fire was thrown into the sea. This may be a giant meteor that crashes into the ocean, one third of the sea turns to blood, one third of the creatures in the sea are killed and one third of the ships are destroyed. This is God's judgment on the sea. The third trumpet causes a star on fire to fall onto the rivers and springs, the name given to the star is Wormwood. Wormwood is absinth and it is known for its bitterness, this will contaminate the fresh water, and it is God's judgment on the fresh waters. When the fourth trumpet sounds one third of the sun, moon and stars are darkened. This may be something in the atmosphere that blocks out the light, something similar happened back in 1816. A volcano called Mount Tambora erupted in April of 1815, vast amounts of volcanic ash were ejected into the atmosphere, the ash filtered the sunlight and caused global temperatures to drop 0.7-1.3°. A large volcanic eruption would cause the sky to be filled with ash and dim the light of the sun, moon and stars. This is just a guess, only God knows how He will accomplish this judgment. This is God's judgment on the sky. These first four judgments have already been bad, one third of the land, sea, fresh water and the light have been destroyed, an eagle warns about the final three trumpets.

The fifth angel sounded his trumpet, and I saw a star that had fallen from the sky to the earth. The star was given the key to the shaft of the Abyss. 2 When he opened the Abyss, smoke rose from it like the smoke from a gigantic furnace. The sun and sky were darkened by the smoke from the Abyss. 3 And out of the smoke locusts came down on the earth and were given power like that of scorpions of the earth. 4 They were told not to harm the grass of the earth or any plant or tree, but only those people who did not have the seal of God on their foreheads. 5 They were not allowed to kill them but only to torture them for five months. And the agony they suffered was like that of the sting of a scorpion when it strikes. 6 During those days people will seek death but will not find it; they will long to die, but death will elude them. 7 The locusts looked like horses prepared for battle. On their heads they wore something like crowns of gold, and their faces resembled human faces. 8 Their hair was like women's hair, and their teeth were like lions' teeth. 9 They had breastplates like breastplates of iron, and the sound of their wings was like the thundering of many horses and chariots rushing into battle. 10 They had tails with stingers, like scorpions, and in their tails they had power to torment people for five months. 11 They had as king over them the angel of the Abyss, whose name in Hebrew is Abaddon and in Greek is Apollyon (that is, Destroyer). 12 The first woe is past; two other woes are yet to come. 13 The sixth angel sounded his trumpet, and I heard a voice coming from the four horns of the golden altar that is before God. 14 It said to the sixth angel who had the trumpet, "Release the four angels who are bound at the great river Euphrates." 15 And the four angels who had been kept ready for this very hour and day and month and year were released to kill a third of mankind. 16 The number of the mounted troops was twice ten thousand times ten thousand. I heard their number. 17 The horses and riders I saw in my vision looked like this: Their breastplates were fiery red, dark blue, and yellow as sulfur. The heads of the horses resembled the heads of lions, and out of their mouths came fire, smoke and sulfur. 18 A third of mankind was killed by the three plagues of fire, smoke and sulfur *that came out of their mouths. 19 The power of the horses was in their mouths and in their tails; for their tails were like snakes, having heads with which they inflict injury. 20 The rest of mankind who were not killed by these plagues still did not repent of the work of their hands; they did not stop worshiping demons, and idols of gold, silver, bronze, stone and wood—idols that cannot see or hear or walk. 21 Nor did they repent of their murders, their magic arts, their sexual immorality or their thefts. Revelation 9:1-20*

When the fifth trumpet sounds an angel comes down to open the key to the abyss. Smoke pours out of the abyss and releases demonic entities; these entities were told they could sting anyone that did not have God's mark on their forehead. Now you may wonder why God is releasing these creatures, since they are demonic, God is only releasing them from the abyss as a judgment. They enjoy stinging people but God gives them parameters, they cannot kill anyone and they are not to touch those that God has marked as His own. They are led by Apollyon or Abaddon, an arch-demon whose name means destruction. Once these demonic creatures sting someone the person is in so much pain and agony that they want to die but they can't. Once a person is stung the pain will last for five months. John describes what these demonic creatures look like. They looked like horses prepared for battle; they were well prepared for their mission. They wore crowns of gold; this symbolizes the fact that they will be victorious in their mission. Their faces resembled human faces; you can see the cunning and intelligence in their expressions. They had hair like women's hair; some ancient warriors wore their hair long as a symbol of fierceness. They had teeth like a lions' teeth, another symbol for fierceness. They had breastplates of iron, they were invincible. The sound of their wings is like the thundering of many horses, in ancient wars the participants made as much noise as possible to intimidate their foes. They had tails and stings like scorpions, they were supernatural beings.When the sixth angel blows his trumpet a voice by the altar of God commands the four angels who are bound at the Euphrates River to be released. These are fallen angels that will lead a demonic army and are allowed to kill one third of mankind. They lead an army of two hundred million, described by John to be wearing breastplates of red, blue and yellow, this represents the red of fire, the blue of smoke and the yellow of sulfur. The breastplates symbolize their invincibility and the plagues of fire, smoke and sulfur that they bring. The heads of the horse's resembled lion's heads, a lion is terrifying when it attacks. Out of their mouths came fire, smoke and sulfur, a deadly attack. Their tails were like snakes, with biting heads. One third of mankind is killed by these demons. The other two thirds refuse to repent.

3 And I will appoint my two witnesses, and they will prophesy for 1,260 days, clothed in sackcloth." 4 They are "the two olive trees" and the two lampstands, and "they stand before the Lord of the earth." 5 If anyone tries to harm them, fire comes from their mouths and devours their enemies. This is how anyone who wants to harm them must die.6 They have power to shut up the heavens so that it will not rain during the time they are prophesying; and they have power to turn the waters into blood and to strike the earth with every kind of plague as often as they want. 7 Now when they have finished their testimony, the beast that comes up from the Abyss will attack them, and overpower and kill them. 8 Their bodies will lie in the public square of the great city—which is figuratively called Sodom and Egypt—where also their Lord was crucified. 9 For three and a half days some from every people, tribe, language and nation will gaze on their bodies and refuse them burial. 10 The inhabitants of the earth will gloat over them and will celebrate by sending each other gifts, because these two prophets had tormented those who live on the earth. 11 But after the three and a half days the breath[b] of life from God entered them, and they stood on their feet, and terror struck those who saw them.12 Then they heard a loud voice from heaven saying to them,

"Come up here." And they went up to heaven in a cloud, while their enemies looked on. 13 At that very hour there was a severe earthquake and a tenth of the city collapsed. Seven thousand people were killed in the earthquake, and the survivors were terrified and gave glory to the God of heaven. Revelation 11:3-13

Before the final trumpet is blown the Bible talks about the two witnesses. No one knows who these witnesses are, but many think they will be Moses and Elijah because they appeared with Jesus when he was transfigured and taken up to heaven. They will prophesy in Israel for 1260 days wearing sackcloth, a coarse fabric made of goat's hair. Anyone that tries to harm them will be killed with fire that comes from their mouths. During the time that they are prophesying they can cause no rains to fall, turn water to blood and cause plague. They will prophesy for the first half of the Tribulation, or three and a half years, after this time they will be killed. For three and a half days their bodies will lie dead while everyone celebrates their death. They celebrate too soon because God raises them back to life and takes them to heaven, the people look on with terror. Then God causes a massive earthquake and one tenth of the city collapses. Seven thousand are killed in this earthquake. The seventh trumpet releases the bowl or vial judgments. At the blast of the trumpet there is an announcement in heaven that the earth now belongs to God. In the beginning, God gave dominion of the earth to Adam. When Adam sinned, dominion passed to Satan who has ruled the earth since that time, but God now takes dominion back. At this point there is a storm in heaven to signify that the first half of the Tribulation is over and the Great Tribulation, the final three and a half years are about to begin. At the end of this time Jesus will return to earth for the final battle where Satan will be defeated.

15 The seventh angel sounded his trumpet, and there were loud voices in heaven, which said: "The kingdom of the world has become the kingdom of our Lord and of his Messiah, and he will reign for ever and ever." 16 And the twenty-four elders, who were seated on their thrones before God, fell on their faces and worshiped God, 17 saying: "We give thanks to you, Lord God Almighty, the One who is and who was, because you have taken your great power and have begun to reign. 18 The nations were angry, and your wrath has come. The time has come for judging the dead, and for rewarding your servants the prophets and your people who revere your name, both great and small—and for destroying those who destroy the earth." 19 Then God's temple in heaven was opened, and within his temple was seen the ark of his covenant. And there came flashes of lightning, rumblings, peals of thunder, an earthquake and a severe hailstorm. Revelation 11:15-19

The Seven Bowls

We have reached the midpoint of the Tribulation. Three
and a half years are done and there are three and a half
more to go. The next half of the Tribulation is known as the
Great Tribulation and if you thought the first half was bad
these last years are going to be so much worse. The event
that begins the Great Tribulation is when the Antichrist
enters the rebuilt Jewish Temple and claims that he is god.

*14 "When you see 'the abomination that causes
desolation' standing where it does not belong—let the
reader understand—then let those who are in Judea flee to
the mountains. Mark 13:14 (NIV) 27 He will confirm a
covenant with many for one 'seven.' In the middle of the
'seven' he will put an end to sacrifice and offering. And at
the temple he will set up an abomination that causes
desolation, until the end that is decreed is poured out on
him." Daniel 9:27 (NIV)*

*3 Don't let anyone deceive you in any way, for that day
will not come until the rebellion occurs and the man of
lawlessness is revealed, the man doomed to destruction. 4
He will oppose and will exalt himself over everything that is
called God or is worshiped, so that he sets himself up in*

God's temple, proclaiming himself to be God. 2 Thessalonians 2:3-4 (NIV)

The Temple will be rebuilt in the beginning of the Tribulation period. I don't know how this will happen, it could be that the Dome of the Rock is destroyed, it could be that they find that the real site of the Temple is not in the same spot as the mosque, it could be anything. I have a possible idea that the War of Gog and Magog may take place right before the treaty is signed or just after. There will be a surprise attack on Israel. They will not be able to defend themselves but God will miraculously destroy all the enemies that come against them. It may be at this point that the Dome of the Rock is destroyed. There is no prophetic event in the Bible that takes place before this attack, so it may come before the rapture or after.

The word of the LORD came to me: 2 "Son of man, set your face against Gog, of the land of Magog, the chief prince of Meshek and Tubal; prophesy against him 3 and say: 'This is what the Sovereign LORD says: I am against you, Gog, chief prince of Meshek and Tubal. 4 I will turn you around, put hooks in your jaws and bring you out with your whole army—your horses, your horsemen fully armed, and a great horde with large and small shields, all of them brandishing their swords. 5 Persia, Cush and Put will be with them, all with shields and helmets, 6 also Gomer with all its troops, and Beth Togarmah from the far north with all its troops—the many nations with you. 7 "'Get ready; be prepared, you and all the hordes gathered about you, and take command of them. 8 After many days you will be called to arms. In future years you will invade a land that has recovered from war, whose people were gathered from many nations to the mountains of Israel, which had long been desolate. They had been brought out from the nations, and now all of them live in safety. 9 You and all your troops and the many nations with you will go up, advancing like a storm; you will be like a cloud covering the land.10 "'This is what the Sovereign LORD says: On that day thoughts will come into your mind and you will devise an evil scheme. 11 You will say, "I will invade a land of unwalled villages; I will attack a peaceful and unsuspecting people—all of them living without walls and without gates and bars. 12 I will plunder and loot and turn my hand against the resettled ruins and the people gathered from the nations, rich in livestock and goods, living at the center of the land."13 Sheba and Dedan and the merchants of Tarshish and all her villages will say to you, "Have you come to plunder? Have you gathered your hordes to loot, to carry off silver and gold, to take away livestock and goods and to seize much plunder?"' 14 "Therefore, son of man, prophesy and say to Gog: 'This is what the Sovereign

LORD says: In that day, when my people Israel are living in safety, will you not take notice of it? 15 You will come from your place in the far north, you and many nations with you, all of them riding on horses, a great horde, a mighty army. 16 You will advance against my people Israel like a cloud that covers the land. In days to come, Gog, I will bring you against my land, so that the nations may know me when I am proved holy through you before their eyes. 17 "'This is what the Sovereign LORD says: You are the one I spoke of in former days by my servants the prophets of Israel. At that time they prophesied for years that I would bring you against them. 18 This is what will happen in that day: When Gog attacks the land of Israel, my hot anger will be aroused, declares the Sovereign LORD. 19 In my zeal and fiery wrath I declare that at that time there shall be a great earthquake in the land of Israel. 20 The fish in the sea, the birds in the sky, the beasts of the field, every creature that moves along the ground, and all the people on the face of the earth will tremble at my presence. The mountains will be overturned, the cliffs will crumble and every wall will fall to the ground. 21 I will summon a sword against Gog on all my mountains, declares the Sovereign LORD. Every man's sword will be against his brother. 22 I will execute judgment on him with plague and bloodshed; I will pour down torrents of rain, hailstones and burning sulfur on him and on his troops and on the many nations with him. 23 And so I will show my greatness and my holiness, and I will make myself known in the sight of many nations. Then they will know that I am the LORD.' Ezekiel 38:1-23

You may wonder who these nations are that will attack Israel. They don't sound like any countries that exist today. To figure this out you need to go back to the time of Noah, now Noah had three sons Ham, Shem and Japheth. Now Shem was the ancestor of the Semitic peoples, the middle eastern people including Israel. Japheth was the ancestor of Gomer, Magog, Tarshish, Meshech, and Tubal. Ham was the ancestor of Cush, Sheba, Dedan, and Put. If you study ancient maps you can see where these peoples settled. This is a list of the peoples that Ezekiel prophesied against and the current country names.

Gog of Magog would be Russia

Meshek would be the Former Soviet States

Tubal would be Georgia

Persia would be Iran, Iraq, Afghanistan

Cush would be Sudan, Ethiopia

Put would be Libya

Gomer would be Eastern Europe

Beth Togarmah would be Turkey

No one will come to Israel's aid when they are attacked, not even the United States. It could be that the other countries are unable to help Israel because of events that happen in these countries, we won't know until this takes place. Israel has nothing to fear from this massive attack, God will defend her and miraculously destroy all her enemies and rain down fire and hail on the countries themselves. If you read the list of nations, most of these are Muslim nations, and if God destroys them there would be few Muslims left and no impediment to Israel taking down the mosque and replacing it with their Temple. I don't know if this is how it will happen, but it is a possibility, only God knows for sure. Now we have talked about the Antichrist, but he has a helper, the False Prophet. In the Bible it says that he rises up out of the earth, when the Bible talks about the earth it is usually talking about Israel; it may be that this False Prophet is a Jew. This man becomes the leader of the one world religion; he even is given power to have fire come down from the sky. Before the Antichrist goes to the Temple and declares that he is god someone tries to assassinate him. He has a head wound and it seems that he is dead, after three days he will rise from the dead but he will be taken over by Satan. At this point the False Prophet will declare that the Antichrist is god and that all should worship him, he was dead and came to life. Statues are built of this man and everyone is required to worship the statue of the Antichrist. The Antichrist has given up all pretense of being peaceful and instead he now declares all-out war on the Jews and any people that are believers in God. The False Prophet institutes a new system where everyone has to be marked to be able to buy or sell. I am sure that you have heard of the mark of the beast or the number of his name, 666. In this new system, everyone will need to have this mark on their right hand or their forehead. Now I don't know how this system will be implemented, will there be a microchip implanted in your skin or will it be a tattoo that is scanable, there could even be a new technology for this mark. Anyone that is found without the mark and who refuses to take it and worship the Antichrist will be put to death.

11 Then I saw a second beast, coming out of the earth. It had two horns like a lamb, but it spoke like a dragon. 12 It exercised all the authority of the first beast on its behalf, and made the earth and its inhabitants worship the first beast, whose fatal wound had been healed. 13 And it performed great signs, even causing fire to come down from heaven to the earth in full view of the people. 14 Because of the signs it was given power to perform on behalf of the first beast, it deceived the inhabitants of the earth. It ordered them to set up an image in honor of the beast who was wounded by the sword and yet lived.15

*The second beast was given power to give breath to the
image of the first beast, so that the image could speak and
cause all who refused to worship the image to be killed. 16
It also forced all people, great and small, rich and poor,
free and slave, to receive a mark on their right hands or on
their foreheads, 17 so that they could not buy or sell unless
they had the mark, which is the name of the beast or the
number of its name. 18 This calls for wisdom. Let the
person who has insight calculate the number of the beast,
for it is the number of a man. That number is 666.
Revelation 13:11-18 (NIV)*

    Now that the stage is set, the final judgments will be
poured out on the earth. After these last judgments are
completed God's wrath on earth will be finished and Jesus
will return. The final seven bowls of wrath are given to
seven angels to be poured onto the earth. The first angel
pours out his bowl on the land and everyone that has the
mark of the beast and has worshipped the statue of the
beast breaks out with rotting sores. The second angel
pours out his bowl on the sea, the sea turns to blood and
every living creature in the sea dies. The third angel pours
his bowl onto the rivers and springs and they turn to blood,
there is no clean water to drink. The fourth angel pours his
bowl on the sun, the sun became so hot that it scorched
people with fire; the people cursed God and still refused to

repent. The fifth angel pours his bowl onto the throne of the beast, the place where the Antichrist has his headquarters or his kingdom, the area is plunged into such deep darkness that people feel it like it is painful;. The sixth angel pours his bowl on the Euphrates River and it dries up in preparation for the armies of the east coming for the battle at Armageddon. At this time demonic spirits are sent out to gather all the armies of the world for the great battle that will come. Finally the seventh angel pours out their bowl into the air, from the temple in heaven there is a loud voice saying that "It is done!" There is lightning and thunder and the most severe worldwide earthquake the planet has ever known. All the cities of the nations collapsed, all islands were gone and there were no more mountains and giant hailstones weighing 100 lbs. fell to earth and crushed people.

Then I heard a loud voice from the temple saying to the seven angels, "Go, pour out the seven bowls of God's wrath on the earth." 2 The first angel went and poured out his bowl on the land, and ugly, festering sores broke out on the people who had the mark of the beast and worshiped its image. 3 The second angel poured out his bowl on the sea, and it turned into blood like that of a dead person, and every living thing in the sea died. 4 The third angel poured out his bowl on the rivers and springs of water, and they became blood. 5 Then I heard the angel in charge of the waters say: "You are just in these judgments, O Holy One, you who are and who were;6 for they have shed the blood of your holy people and your prophets, and you have given them blood to drink as they deserve."

7 And I heard the altar respond: "Yes, Lord God Almighty, true and just are your judgments."8 The fourth angel poured out his bowl on the sun, and the sun was allowed to scorch people with fire. 9 They were seared by the intense heat and they cursed the name of God, who had control over these plagues, but they refused to repent and glorify him. 10 The fifth angel poured out his bowl on the throne of the beast, and its kingdom was plunged into darkness. People gnawed their tongues in agony11 and cursed the God of heaven because of their pains and their sores, but they refused to repent of what they had done. 12 The sixth angel poured out his bowl on the great river Euphrates, and its water was dried up to prepare the way for the kings from the East. 13 Then I saw three impure spirits that looked like frogs; they came out of the mouth of the dragon, out of the mouth of the beast and out of the mouth of the false prophet. 14 They are demonic spirits that perform signs, and they go out to the kings of the whole world, to gather them for the battle on the great day of God Almighty. 15 "Look, I come like a thief! Blessed is the one who stays awake and remains clothed, so as not to go naked and be shamefully exposed." 16 Then they gathered the kings together to the place that in Hebrew is called Armageddon. 17 The seventh angel poured out his bowl into the air, and out of the temple came a loud voice from the throne, saying, "It is done!" 18 Then there came flashes of lightning, rumblings, peals of thunder and a severe earthquake. No earthquake like it has ever occurred since mankind has been on earth, so tremendous was the quake. 19 The great city split into three parts, and the cities of the nations collapsed. God remembered Babylon the Great and gave her the cup filled with the wine of the fury of his wrath. 20 Every island fled away and the mountains could not be found. 21 From the sky huge hailstones, each weighing about a hundred pounds fell on people. And they cursed God on account of the plague of hail, because the plague was so terrible. Revelation 16:1-21 (NIV)

What Happens at the End of the Judgments?

The judgments are completed, now the final battle will begin. A white horse appears in heaven, its rider has a bow and is wearing a crown; He goes to conquer. The rider's name is Faithful and True so we know that the rider is Jesus.

14 "To the angel of the church in Laodicea write: These are the words of the Amen, the faithful and true witness, the ruler of God's creation. Revelation 3:14

He judges and wages war with justice; He is the judge of all the earth. His eyes are like blazing fire.

The hair on his head was white like wool, as white as snow, and his eyes were like blazing fire. Revelation 1:14

On His head are many crowns, signifying that He is the King of Kings. There is a name written on Him that no one knows but Himself. He is dressed in a robe dipped in blood

1 Who is this coming from Edom, from Bozrah, with his garments stained crimson? Who is this, robed in splendor, striding forward in the greatness of his strength? "It is I, proclaiming victory, mighty to save." 2 Why are your garments red, like those of one treading the winepress?3 "I have trodden the winepress alone; from the nations no one was with me. I trampled them in my anger and trod them down in my wrath; their blood spattered my garments, and I stained all my clothing. Isaiah 63:1-3

This signifies that the rider is no stranger to battle. His name is the Word of God, referring to the revealed will of God. Christ returning to fight the enemies of God will now be fulfilling the gospel. Behind this rider are the armies of heaven, clothed in linen on white horses. The plural being used for armies would indicate that there is more than one army following Jesus at this time. The first army would be the raptured believers.

14 They will make war against the Lamb, but the Lamb will overcome them because he is Lord of lords and King of kings–and with him will be his called, chosen and faithful followers." Revelation 17:14

The second army will be God's angels

6 God is just: He will pay back trouble to those who trouble you 7 and give relief to you who are troubled, and to us as well. This will happen when the Lord Jesus is revealed from heaven in blazing fire with his powerful angels. 2 Thessalonians 1:6-7

Out of His mouth comes a sharp sword:

12 For the word of God is alive and active. Sharper than any double-edged sword, it penetrates even to dividing soul and spirit, joints and marrow; it judges the thoughts and attitudes of the heart. Hebrews 4:12

So He may strike down nations and rule them with a rod of iron. He treads the winepress of the wrath of God.

17 Another angel came out of the temple in heaven, and he too had a sharp sickle. 18 Still another angel, who had charge of the fire, came from the altar and called in a loud voice to him who had the sharp sickle, "Take your sharp sickle and gather the clusters of grapes from the earth's vine, because its grapes are ripe." 19 The angel swung his sickle on the earth, gathered its grapes and threw them into the great winepress of God's wrath. 20 They were trampled in the winepress outside the city, and blood flowed out of the press, rising as high as the horses' bridles for a distance of 1,600 stadia. Revelation 14:17-20 (NIV)

At this point the battle is over, Jesus has easily won. An angel chains up Satan and seals him into an abyss for one thousand years; the Antichrist and False Prophet are thrown into the lake of fire. Now there is a sheep and goats judgment, all those that lived through the Tribulation period will be judged at this time. All those that did not take the mark of the beast or worship his image and believed in God are the sheep and they are judged as righteous. All those that took the mark of the beast and worshiped his image are thrown into the lake of fire.

31 "When the Son of Man comes in his glory, and all the angels with him, he will sit on his glorious throne. 32 All the nations will be gathered before him, and he will separate the people one from another as a shepherd separates the sheep from the goats. 33 He will put the sheep on his right and the goats on his left. 34 "Then the King will say to those on his right, 'Come, you who are blessed by my Father; take your inheritance, the kingdom prepared for you since the creation of the world. 35 For I was hungry and you gave me something to eat, I was thirsty and you gave me something to drink, I was a stranger and you invited me in, 36 I needed clothes and you clothed me, I was sick and you looked after me, I was in prison and you came to visit me.' 37 "Then the righteous will answer him, 'Lord, when did we see you hungry and feed you, or thirsty and give you something to drink? 38 When did we see you a stranger and invite you in, or needing clothes and clothe you? 39 When did we see you sick or in prison and go to visit you?' 40 "The King will reply, 'Truly I tell you, whatever you did for one of the least of these brothers and sisters of mine, you did for me.' 41 "Then he will say to those on his left, 'Depart from me, you who are cursed, into the eternal fire prepared for the devil and his angels. 42 For I was hungry and you gave me nothing to eat, I was thirsty and you gave me nothing to drink, 43 I was a stranger and you did not invite me in, I needed clothes and you did not clothe me, I was sick and in prison and you did not look after me.' 44 "They also will answer, 'Lord, when did we see you hungry or thirsty or a stranger or needing clothes or sick or in prison, and did not help you?' 45 "He will reply, 'Truly I tell you, whatever you did not do for one of the least of these, you did not do for me.' 46 "Then they will go away to eternal punishment, but the righteous to eternal life." Matthew 25:31-46 (NIV)

Now Jesus will reign on earth, a cleansed earth for one thousand years. All those that were judged as sheep will pass into this millennium period and live in a world without Satan. Those that were martyred or raptured will rule and reign with Jesus during this time. After the thousand years is almost over, Satan is let loose for a short time, he gathers up nations to battle Jesus and once more Jesus will defeat him and this time he will be thrown into the lake of fire forever. Now you may wonder how Satan was able to gather up these armies in a world where everyone can see Jesus ruling. There will always be those that want to rebel against any kind of authority. After this final battle the final judgment will take place, the Great White Throne judgment. All those that have died as unbelievers will be judged according to their works. Their names will not be in the Book of Life and they will be judged for their sins and thrown into the lake of fire.

11 Then I saw a great white throne and him who was seated on it. The earth and the heavens fled from his presence, and there was no place for them.12 And I saw the dead, great and small, standing before the throne, and books were opened. Another book was opened, which is the book of life. The dead were judged according to what they had done as recorded in the books. 13 The sea gave up the dead that were in it, and death and Hades gave up the dead that were in them, and each person was judged according to what they had done. 14 Then death and Hades were thrown into the lake of fire. The lake of fire is the second death. 15 Anyone whose name was not found written in the book of life was thrown into the lake of fire. Revelation 20:11-15

All those that were raptured and martyred and lived through the millennial period trusting God will now live in the new heaven and the new earth. God will dwell among us.

Then I saw "a new heaven and a new earth," for the first heaven and the first earth had passed away, and there was no longer any sea. 2 I saw the Holy City, the new Jerusalem, coming down out of heaven from God, prepared as a bride beautifully dressed for her husband. 3 And I heard a loud voice from the throne saying, "Look! God's dwelling place is now among the people, and he will dwell with them. They will be his people, and God himself will be with them and be their God. 4 'He will wipe every tear from their eyes. There will be no more death' or mourning or crying or pain, for the old order of things has passed away." Revelation 21:1-4

So hold firmly to your belief in God. The trials and tribulations that you will have to endure will only last a short while and then you will have eternal life without any more pain or sadness. Whether you are a seeker or you have been left behind these words are true and there is still hope for you. If the rapture has not occurred yet there is still time to get right with God and avoid the tribulations that will come. God has given you free will, it is your choice; He is offering you the free gift of salvation that He paid for you with His blood. He loved you so much that He was willing to die in the most painful and shameful way so that you would be able to be saved from your sin. We are all sinners, we are born as sinners because of Adam's choice in the Garden of Eden, but because of Jesus we do not have to die for our sins.

23 for all have sinned and fall short of the glory of God, 24 and all are justified freely by his grace through the redemption that came by Christ Jesus. 25 God presented Christ as a sacrifice of atonement, through the shedding of his blood—to be received by faith. He did this to demonstrate his righteousness, because in his forbearance he had left the sins committed beforehand unpunished— 26 he did it to demonstrate his righteousness at the present time, so as to be just and the one who justifies those who have faith in Jesus. Romans 3:23-26 (NIV)

If you are feeling that you want to make a commitment to follow Jesus but you don't know what to say, you can pray this simple prayer and Jesus will accept you into His family. I urge you to make the choice to follow Jesus, there is no other way to avoid the coming Tribulation and no other way to eternal life.

Heavenly Father, in Jesus' name I confess that I have sinned and ask for forgiveness. I ask that Jesus come into my heart and become my Lord and Savior. I believe Jesus died for my sins and was raised from the dead. Thank You Father for saving me in Jesus' name. Amen.

Maranatha- Come Lord Jesus

Rapture Survival Kit

When the mark of the beast is implemented you will not be able to buy or sell without the mark. No one should take the mark! Once you have taken it you are showing your allegiance to the beast, there is no going back. The best thing to do is to prepare now for this time. This is a modified earthquake survival list, but while an earthquake kit only needs to help you get through a few days to a week before help arrives, this kit is for a more long term survival. Now that you have read through this book and know what to expect you need to start planning for your survival. I am giving you a basic list of what you may need but you should really take some time and think about what other items you can use to help you to survive. Always have a go bag ready with basic supplies in case a disaster or something happens where you need to get away quickly.

•Acquire non-perishable foodstuffs that will not go bad and stockpile them.

•Create an indoor garden to grow fresh fruits and vegetables

•Gold is always of value and you may be able to trade it for supplies or other necessities

•If you can find a remote place to live you can forage off the land

•If you do decide to live off the land, head to a bookstore and gather some books on wilderness survival and edible plant life.

•Weapons will be needed to protect yourselves from animals and human gangs or mobs, do not use guns for hunting, you do not want to draw attention to yourself.

•Communications equipment that is not traceable, there should be kits available to scramble communications

•Water will be necessary, acquire water purification tablets or bleach (8-16 drops of bleach for 1 gallon of water, double the amount if water is cloudy, shake and let stand for 30 minutes)

•Medical supplies will also be necessary since you will not be able to go to a hospital without the mark, collect basic medical supplies and antibiotics if you can get them

•You will need Bibles to continue learning and to keep track of the judgments, at some point it will become illegal to own a Bible. Create stockpiles before this happens; bury them in waterproof packaging in as many areas as possible.

•Equipment to keep abreast of what is happening in the world, a TV, a radio, a computer (you can get a crank radio)

•Clothing, shoes, blankets, tarps and sleeping bags for all seasons

•Hygiene supplies like soap

•Duct tape has many uses

•A good knife

•Tools

•A light source (candles, matches, lanterns, flashlights)

•Solar charger, you can charge small electronics on these

###

Thank you for reading my book. I hope that you learned something from it and that you have made a commitment to follow Jesus. I am praying for all those that read this book.

Maranatha!

L. Bohm

Subscribe to my blog:

https://endtimebibleprophecyblog.wordpress.com/

Made in United States
Cleveland, OH
10 December 2024